MOON SPELLS

AN ENCHANTING SPELL BOOK OF MAGIC & RITUALS

Aurora Kane

wellfleet
press

Introduction

For centuries, the Moon has been an object of fascination. To this day, her luminescence has a mysterious hold on all of us. We have relied on her for telling the time and giving us information about the ocean's current. Some of us are even hormonally affected by the Moon, causing us to have mood swings in time with the Full Moon. She's a powerful force who subtly pulls on us, and we move with her, whether we realize it or not. She has been and continues to be a massive presence in our lives.

Several religions throughout history have recognized the Moon as a deity and worshipped her, not only with rituals but with offerings and prayer. Out of this devotion and reverence comes Moon magic. Moon magic is the practice of working alongside the Moon's phases and using them as a guide for spellwork. It's about tuning in to the natural rhythms of the earth and working from there. The Sun and Moon work together to create the Moon's cycles, appealing to us at all times of the day. It results in a truly spectacular form of magic.

To work with the Moon, we must recognize her nine phases: Dark Moon, New Moon, Waxing Crescent, First Quarter, Waxing Gibbous, Full Moon, Waning Gibbous, Last Quarter, and Waning Crescent. In that order, the Moon goes from her sleeping phase to her brightest to quieting down and then back to sleep. The Moon has lived millions of lives throughout humanity's existence. Each new life brings new challenges, victories, and magic.

Communicating with the Moon means asking her for what you want by using rituals and spells. A spell is casting your word upon the world. A Moon spell is casting your will with the help of the Moon. A Moon ritual is a set of tasks to help get yourself in the right headspace to work alongside the Moon and using her energies to get what you desire. It's a joint effort stemming from respect. Each phase of the Moon has its own specialties, so to speak, and each spell has an ideal phase in which to perform it.

The Moon works in roughly four distinct phases. Chapter 1 covers the Dark Moon and the New Moon phases. This is the time when witches can rest and begin again, similar to someone being born or getting a fresh start. It's a time for spells and rituals about rest, rejuvenation, and then forward motion. Dream big, and don't let anything stop you.

Chapter 2 covers the three-part phase of the Waxing Crescent, First Quarter, and Waxing Gibbous Moons. It is a period of growth and action. This is when the light of the Sun starts to illuminate the Moon. It's a time of new beginnings that are more concrete than the New Moon phase. Instead of dreaming of the possibilities, you create them. Here, you build a path for yourself to get what you want and conduct your magic to help you along. It's an exciting time in which you're making decisions to improve your life.

The next phase is the Full Moon. Some would argue this is the best time of the Moon's cycle, and they wouldn't necessarily be wrong. The Full Moon is when the Moon is at her brightest, which means she's also at her most powerful. It's no wonder she gets much of the attention in witchcraft and in the media. There's nothing like a bright, yellow Full Moon. She commands attention because of her beauty and resplendence. This time of the month is perfect for any spell you can think of; it's when spells will be the most effective. Chapter 3 is all about utilizing this influence and high energy.

The fourth and final phase is the intermixture of the Waning Gibbous, Last Quarter, and Waning Crescent Moons. This is when, ideally, all you wanted to accomplish for the month has happened and now you're meant to slow down and reap the rewards. This lunar cycle has a slightly negative connotation because the best of the month is gone and we watch the Moon weaken before our eyes. But that's not the right way to think of it! Instead, the Moon has served her purpose, and now all that's left to do is reflect on what's occurred, learn from it, and relax. If the Moon has to do it, so do we. Chapter 4 covers this crucial stage of rumination, protection, and release.

No matter what phase the Moon is in, you will find what you need to capitalize on her power in these pages. Feel free to combine, cut, or personalize these spells to your liking. The relationship between you and Mother Moon is unique, and that relationship should be reflected in your spellwork. Ask and receive.

SO MOTE IT BE.*

*The term "So mote it be" used within is a ritual phrase historically used by Freemasons, and currently used by Neopagan practitioners translated to mean "so it must be."

1
New Moon Spells

THE NEW MOON PHASE, ALSO known as the Maiden phase or the Black Moon phase, is the genesis of the Moon's journey. It's when she's wiped clean before beginning her ascent to full actualization. Everything is new, young, hopeful, and full of potential, just like spring. This is when you can return to a state of whimsy, dreaming, and hope, starting fresh and going back to your roots. In this chapter, you'll clarify your goals, learn to do shadow work, and shake off the past from the last Moon cycle. Let your imagination run wild!

What people refer to as the New Moon is actually two phases of the Moon combined—the Dark Moon and the New Moon. The Dark Moon isn't typically discussed, partly because it sounds a little foreboding. But the Dark Moon isn't to be feared. Instead, this should be thought of as the Moon's rest period. It's when she is the darkest and disappears entirely from the night sky. For magical purposes, this is the time for slumber and contemplation, when there's peace and quiet to prepare for the New Moon and her energies.

The New Moon is the short period in which the Moon starts to become illuminated. Once she's awake, she jumps right into action, and so do we. New Moon spells typically revolve around setting goals for yourself, making personal changes to your life, and new beginnings as a whole. It's a time of potential, planning, and new adventures. This is partly why the New Moon gets more attention than the Dark Moon. She's overtly positive and is ready to help you in your future endeavors.

Here, you will learn how to conquer the changes in your life that might shake your confidence. You'll find ways to attract new things into your life, such as increased earnings, a new home, or a new job. You'll navigate your way through issues such as fertility, work with Mother Moon directly, and experience shadow work—facing your dark side.

Conquering Change

New beginnings are times of change, and times of change can shake even the most confident of us. To help, try this spell during the next Black Moon phase.

1. Gather a yellow candle and a tiger's eye crystal.

2. Sit quietly somewhere comfortable, place the candle on a heatproof surface, light it, and imagine yourself acting with confidence and purpose.

3. Hold the tiger's eye in your dominant hand. Focus on the flame and feel it illuminate your soul.

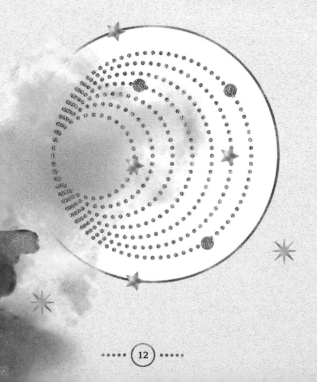

4. Calling on the Black Moon's quiet power, say quietly or aloud:

Spell

O' quiet Moon, guide my thoughts,
as I cast aside my fears and doubts.
Fill me instead with peace and resolve,
as I feel my confidence grow and evolve.
This tiger's eye I have in hand,
reminds me of how change demands.
I sit here, still and thankfully,
blessed for all eternity.

5. Sit quietly for a few minutes when finished, feeling quiet confidence swell inside you. Really feel the emotion, knowing you can recapture it anytime you need it.

Money Luck

The New Moon is a good time for new beginnings and setting wheels in motion, so try this simple spell for increased earnings.

According to the laws of the Universe, getting more starts with giving more, and giving starts with gratitude. First give thanks for what you have. Take a moment to reflect and set an intention to share your wealth–be it money or talents–with the Universe.

Spell

My simple wealth is made of happiness, love, and health.
I have talents to share to help others.
I will make time to give back to the Universe.

Once you've aligned yourself with gratitude, cast this simple spell.

1. Gather a few pennies in your hand.

2. Go outside, if you can, and stand under the Moon, absorbing its cleansing energy. Feel yourself letting go of any blocking negativity with each breath out. Open your mind to new opportunities with each breath in. Light a candle, if you wish; a white or silver candle works best. Visualize the wealth you desire.

3. When you are ready, say quietly or aloud:

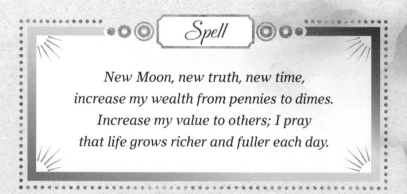

Spell

New Moon, new truth, new time,
increase my wealth from pennies to dimes.
Increase my value to others; I pray
that life grows richer and fuller each day.

Take a moment to give thanks to the New Moon's growing wisdom. Bury the pennies in the ground, if you are able, or tuck them away in a dark space and leave them there.

Finding the Perfect Home

This phase of new beginnings is the perfect time to set an intention for finding that new home you've been dreaming of. Kick the dreaming to the curb, and take action to make it happen. When the New Moon beckons, set aside some time to bask in her energy and say quietly or aloud:

Spell

New Moon, new day, new house I pray,
My search is not yet done.
New Moon, new day, new nest I pray,
Where heart and hearth are one.
New Moon, new day, reveal I pray
That castle I'll call home.

Long Life

It goes so fast and we want it to last forever, but know that the best life–no matter how long–is one lived in the moment each day. Using the latent energy of the New Moon to cast this spell, say quietly or aloud:

Spell

New Moon, walk with me on this journey.
May your ever-steady presence remind me of this promise:
To fill each day with love that fills my life with joy, so, come the day
good-bye I say, I'll have lived life to its fullest.

Finding Inspiration

The Moon has inspired more things than you could even list. Do you think she might be willing to share a little of that? Say quietly or aloud:

Spell

To gaze upon your lovely face is said to bring desire,
from which, it's said, of heart and head you readily inspire.
Please turn your gaze upon my life to quicken its desire
to find the words, or thoughts, or ways to create again untired.

Planning a Vacation

You can turn a Moon dance into a party, but sometimes a vacation can rejuvenate like nothing else. Say quietly or aloud:

Spell

New Moon, you travel through the sky, across its endless seas.
With map I stand, without a plan, but journey beckons me.
A spark ignite–to set aglow ideas that will inspire–
to pack a bag and venture forth with curious desire.

Welcoming Abundance

An abundant life can mean different things—friends, love, money, or learning, for example. Whatever abundance you want to invite in today, whisper this to the New Moon—and remember, everything comes to you as you need it, so be patient:

Spell

So starts your phase from New to Full, and brightly you do grow.
Imbue my world with bounty full and riches by the hour.

Grounding Meditation

As the New Moon begins her growth through a new phase, take the opportunity to ground yourself both in her balancing effects and in the Earth's energy to be truly present in your life.

If you have one, garnet is a great stone to use for its grounding energies. Hold it while sitting or standing comfortably within view of the Moon, close your eyes, and open your mind to the Moon's stabilizing force. Feel your connection to the ground under your feet or the chair in which you sit. Let yourself relax and sink deep into that connection. When you are ready, say quietly or aloud:

Spell

I seek a place to set my roots to deepen as they grow,
To feel the ground beneath my feet and in the present know
That with my strength and clarity, the heavens I may reach.
To use my gifts for all their worth, dear Moon, I do beseech.

Fertile Cauldron

The cauldron, traditional symbol of the hearth, also represents the womb, fertility, transformation, and rebirth. If your wish is to become pregnant, there is no better tool to incorporate into your magic. Along with your cauldron, gather a green candle, matches, water (set nearby for fire safety), and herbs to promote lust (for fun) and fertility (for your wish) such as acorns, apple blossom, cilantro, dill, geranium, ginseng, ivy, lady's mantle, and parsley.

Time your spell to the New Moon, cast it on a Monday, and invite your favorite goddess (Venus is a good choice) to join. Set the cauldron on a heatproof surface and place the candle and herbs next to it. Light the candle. Take a moment to visualize your new little one and how it will feel to hold your baby.

When you are ready, drop the herbs into the cauldron one at a time and say, quietly or aloud and repeating as needed until all the herbs are used:

Spell

The fertile Earth has given birth to each and every herb.
With powers ripe to stir new life—each bloom, each leaf, and seed—
within the Earth to bloom again as much as within me.
O' Moon and goddess, do unite to grant my wish indeed.

Himalayan Salt Ritual

Himalayan salt is actually a crystal—one fully infused with ancient vibrational energies of the oceans and Earth, where it has been growing for more than 250 million years. It is a powerful tool for raising your personal vibrations and contains more than eighty trace elements and minerals that our bodies need. Its vibrational properties are similar to rose quartz, and it offers cleansing and protection from negative energies.

Whether sprinkled on a homemade cookie, or scattered in a bath to soothe and calm, Himalayan salt from the Earth below combined with the Moon's vast wisdom from the sky above creates a magical recipe. Whatever ritual you choose, look to the Moon and, when you are ready, say quietly or aloud:

Spell

Heal, protect, and energize, this salt of Earthly stores
That life tastes fresh and new and best when each day is adored.
I hear the music laugh and play, a message from the Moon.
She says, today do not delay; dance to life and love's sweet tune.

Sharing Your Light

This visualization will connect you with your internal light and guide you to shine it outward.

1. Sit or lie down somewhere comfortable and quiet.

2. Close your eyes and breathe in deeply through your nose, down into your belly, and out of your mouth. Repeat this breathing cycle until you feel present in the moment.

3. Imagine a vibrant pink light entering your body through the top of your head. See this light fill your entire body. Feel the power and beauty of the light.

4. Now visualize this light radiating out of your body until it envelops you, then your room, then your home, and then your neighborhood. Imagine the light surrounding your neighbors and making them feel energetic, happy, and peaceful.

5. Keep envisioning this light growing and wrapping around the people of your town, then your country, and then the globe. Imagine that each person the light touches feels loved. Imagine the feeling that would take over the planet if each person were wrapped in your love light.

6. When you are ready, slowly open your eyes.

Connecting to the Divine Feminine

This New Moon ritual will connect you with the divine feminine energy that is already inside of you.

1. Sit somewhere comfortable, close your eyes, and slowly breathe in and out until you feel yourself relax.

2. Imagine a beautiful goddess standing before you. See her in vivid detail. Notice the way you feel while gazing at her.

3. Now imagine a bright white light radiating from the goddess. This light is her divine feminine energy. Watch it grow until it surrounds you. Let yourself feel its strength, warmth, unconditional love, maternal protection, sensuality, and empathic connection.

4. Now imagine this light filling you. Breathe in and out and open your eyes.

5. Finish by whispering, "I am a goddess."

Banishing Trouble Ritual

New Moon, Full Moon, and Waning Moon phases are the most potent for cleansing energies. When you don't have time for a luxurious Moon bath, use this simple cleansing ritual to meditate your troubles down the drain.

Gather an herbal soap made of herbs corresponding to your intentions.

Take a moment to focus your intentions on what you'd like to rid from your world. Set the tap water in your bathroom sink to run at the perfect temperature to use for washing your face. Gently wash your hands and face with the soap, taking time to acknowledge the soothing scent and give gratitude for the clean water, and then rinse your face and hands while silently visualizing any troubles being washed away.

Attracting Abundance Altar

An altar is a sacred space that is created and dedicated specifically to connect your physical existence with something beyond through ritual. Tapping into the power of the New Moon, you will create an altar to attract abundance.

Pick a space that you see every day, such as your bedside table or your vanity. Or you can choose a space that is out of the way, such as an unused room or a closet shelf.

If you want to use sage or palo santo, light it and allow the smoke to cleanse the space of negativity. When you are ready, state:

Spell

*All negative energy has left this space.
This space is reserved for all things
positive, loving, and true.*

Choose items specific to your definition of financial abundance. You may choose to display a photo of someone you admire who has money acumen, or display items of value you covet, such as a picture of your dream home or a place where you would like to vacation someday.

Incorporate all four elements: fire, earth, water, and air. You can do this by including a candle for fire and air, a small water feature or photo of water, and a crystal for earth.

Get creative when assembling your altar. You are done when you find it inspiring and beautiful.

To bless your altar and activate its power, state:

Spell

This altar is a sacred space.
It assists me with attracting wealth and abundance.
I am grateful to be in sync with this energy
and for the blessings it brings.

New Job Ritual

If you feel the need for a change in your job or career, setting your intentions during the New Moon can bring powerful results. This two-step ritual starts with a bit of meditation, journaling, and soul searching to clarify intentions. The second step simply harnesses the Moon's energy to get your message out into the Universe. Be open to the vibrations and opportunities around you.

1. Gather your journal. Breathe deeply to calm yourself and focus on your thoughts. What do you need to know? Is your job what makes you happy? How do you earn more money? How do you work for a greater good? Let your thoughts work freely on your questions. When you are ready, write down all the thoughts and ideas that came to you.

2. Make three columns—What I Love, What I Can Do, and Which Jobs Use These—and fill in the blanks. You may need to come back to this exercise a number of times before you land on the right path for you.

3. When you have a new job or career goal in mind, it's time to tell the world. Under the light of the New Moon, recite this simple spell, quietly or aloud:

Spell

With open mind and grateful heart, I ask for your support,
As life brings change, to keep my roots but spread my wings apart.
New job, new goals, new intentions set,
Please help me land the job I'm meant
To bring about the change I seek and flourish from the start.

Moon Tea Rite

The soothing warmth of a fragrant cup of tea can restore a worried soul. Following the centuries-old traditions of herbal medicine working to heal what ails, you can concoct a batch of Moon tea and drink it daily to refresh your intentions or just incorporate it as part of your Moon rituals and intention setting. Give thanks to the plants that provide the ingredients for your tea blends and think about how you'll incorporate your tea ritual into intention setting.

A general guideline for making teas is to use 2 to 3 teaspoons of a dried herb or herb blend per cup (8 ounces, or 240 ml) of tea. For larger quantities, say a 1-gallon (3.8 L) jar, that translates to about 1 cup (weight varies) of dried herbs. When you are ready to brew your cup, boil as much Moon water as needed and steep your tea (in a strainer, tea ball, clean unscented muslin bag, or disposable filter) for about 5 minutes.

While the tea steeps, close your eyes and inhale the lovely aromas while you take time to meditate, even if for just a few seconds. Sweeten with dried fruits, spices, honey, or dried culinary flowers, such as rose petal (rose petal and vanilla are delicious together). Strain and serve your Moon tea.

Attracting
New Relationships

The New Moon is all about manifestation. During this phase, anything's on the table. Most of us have solid relationships with those close to us, but maybe you want to invite new people and experiences into your life. Variety is the spice of life, and diversity keeps us knowledgeable and healthy. If you're having trouble making those new connections, the New Moon is the perfect time to call people to you.

What you'll need:

♦ Half an eggshell
♦ Chamomile for happiness the relationships will bring
♦ Rose for love
♦ Clove for attracting love
♦ Dill for manifestation
♦ Daisy for friendship
♦ New Moon water
♦ A spade
♦ A small flowerpot (optional)
♦ Wet dirt (optional)

During the New Moon, carefully place the eggshell somewhere it won't tip over. One by one, add a dash of each herb to the shell. Keep your intention in mind. As you do this, say:

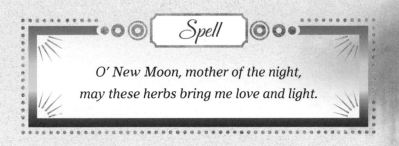

Spell

O' New Moon, mother of the night,
may these herbs bring me love and light.

Take the egg, spade, and Moon water out to your garden or backyard. Find a space to dig a hole for the egg. Do so carefully so that the herbs stay inside the shell. Bury the egg and then pour Moon water over the site to bless it.

If you don't have access to a garden, use a small flowerpot and some dirt. Follow the previous steps, including adding the Moon water. Set the flowerpot on a windowsill that faces the Moon and keep it there until the First Quarter.

Dark Moon Shadow Work

There's a bit of darkness in all of us. Though initially frightening, it isn't anything to be afraid of. The dark side represents the parts of us we dislike, or perhaps a trauma we refuse to deal with. Darkness is necessary and must be embraced if we're to be our true, whole selves. This spell will help you seek out your shadow self and let it teach you the lessons you need to hear.

What you'll need:

♦ Your journal
♦ A mirror with a stand
♦ Smoky quartz for protection, so you feel safe
♦ Bloodstone for honesty
♦ A cloak or a blanket for concealment
♦ A black candle to represent your shadow self
♦ A white candle to represent your current self

Perform this ritual one and a half to three days after the Waning Crescent Moon. This is the short period before the New Moon; it's when the Moon is the darkest she'll be. In your journal, write your negative feelings. Whatever it is you're having a difficult time facing, give words to it. Then, ask your patron deity for support.

Organize your altar and light the black candle. Place the white candle to the right of the black candle. Arrange your mirror so you can see yourself and the black candle. Then, pick up the crystals, putting the smoky quartz in your left hand and the bloodstone in your right. Use the crystals to give you strength and honesty.

Look your reflection in the eyes and think of the things that plague you. See them on your face and how they affect your spirit. You're in control, not your shadow self. No matter how hard it is, don't look away. Face yourself as you are.

Say the words:

Spell

You are a part of me, but you won't destroy me.
I embrace you for what you are, and now you have no power.

Take three deep breaths and sit with yourself until you're on the other side. Thank your deity.

Deep Rest Potion

In life, we go, go, go and don't always afford ourselves the time to stop and rest. There are bills to pay, people to see, and things to do. But we must make time for ourselves. If we're not well-rested, our magic won't be as effective.

As its name might suggest, a Dark Moon occurs when there's no light in the night sky. This is a time of peace and quiet. Now is the time to prioritize rest and rejuvenation.

What you'll need:

- Jasmine for relaxation
- Lavender for calm
- Saffron for Moon magic
- Hibiscus for healing
- A drop of peppermint essential oil for refreshment
- Green jasper for sleep
- Tea steeper

Boil some water and slowly pour it over your steeper into your cup of choice. Taking your time with this forces you to slow down, getting you ready for bed. Swirl your steeper, with the herbs in it, widdershins (counterclockwise) to mimic the Moon's phases moving toward a Dark Moon. As you stir, say aloud:

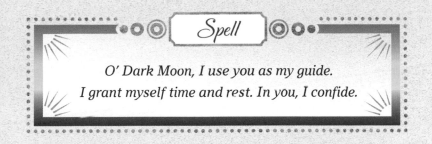

Spell

O' Dark Moon, I use you as my guide.
I grant myself time and rest. In you, I confide.

Let your potion steep for about ten minutes. Add a drop of peppermint oil. Drink the entire cup of tea, and then get ready for bed. Place the green jasper under your pillow as a sleep aid. Goodnight.

Shaking Off the Old and Welcoming the New

Sometimes the month doesn't go as planned. Whether it's unforeseen circumstances, the everyday stress of life, or trouble in our personal lives, we might get caught up in a string of bad luck that feels like it'll never end. When we're stuck and it feels like there's no way out, we can rely on Mother Moon and her powers.

During the Moon's transition from Dark to New, she goes from release and purification to renewal and rejuvenation. And that is precisely what you will do. This spell is for when you want to shake off the remnants of last month and start anew.

What you'll need:

- White candles for purity and new beginnings
- Sea salt for cleansing
- Fennel, sage, and oregano for purification
- A large bay leaf to write on and for banishing
- Your cauldron
- 2 tablespoons (50 g) sand
- A lighter
- A charcoal disk
- A piece of tissue paper big enough to hold the herbs
- Tongs

Set up your altar with white candles and light them. Sprinkle the sea salt to cleanse the altar and the space around you. Place the herbs on the tissue paper and then twist the corners of the paper together so that it seals.

Spread out the sand in the cauldron. Use the tongs to pick up the charcoal disk so that the rounded half is facing out. Light the bottom of the disk until it sparks, and then place it on the sand. Put the tissue paper bundle atop the disk. As the herbs burn, take the cauldron by the handle or with oven mitts and walk about the room widdershins to purify your space.

Next, write down what you want to get rid of from the previous month on the bay leaf. Feel free to write all over the large leaf. When you're done, hold the leaf and pray to Mother Moon that she helps you banish the muck. With the tongs, pick up the leaf and burn it on the flame of the candles. Let it burn out in the cauldron. Take the cauldron to the nearest window where the herbs can burn out safely.

2

Waxing Moon Spells

ONCE THE STARRY-EYED DREAMS of the New Moon have started to form, the Waxing Moon is here to carry them to their next stage. During this time, the ideas of the New Moon phase grow legs, start becoming more detailed, and turn into solid plans. Your dreams are no longer a flight of fancy but now a plan of action. In the following pages, you'll find spells and rituals to help you with luck, your career, and manifesting your dreams.

The Waxing Moon phase is like the start of life. Collectively, it encompasses the Waxing Crescent, the First Quarter, and the Waxing Gibbous Moons. Here are stages of growth in which the Moon progresses toward the Mother stage of her lifespan.

The Waxing Crescent is the time for clarification, money spells, and hope. Just like dipping your toe in the water, the Waxing Crescent is the first taste of making your dreams come true. You're working everything out, trying to fit practical steps to your aspirations, and then acting on them. It can be challenging for those who have trouble planning, but the spells provided in this chapter will guide you.

The First Quarter Moon is a time to build on the action of the previous phase. You've taken your first steps, and now it's time to take more significant action. Here is when you're more sure of yourself and what you're doing because you've made solid progress. During this time, the best spells to perform are about gathering the courage to do more, developing a new skill, luck, or going on a new adventure.

The Waxing Gibbous is the most charged part of this phase. The word *gibbous* refers to swelling, as in growing. It's when the Moon is about to exit maidenhood and cross over to her Mother phase. Now, she's full of energy and can give you the extra push you need to try something new.

Channeling the Magic of Hope

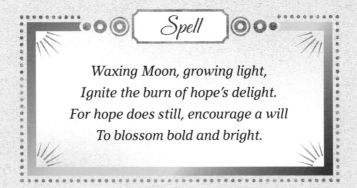

The Waxing Gibbous Moon is full of potential energy in which we can visualize our intentions growing. To keep hope alive and energy flowing, use this simple spell. Say quietly or aloud:

Spell

Waxing Moon, growing light,
Ignite the burn of hope's delight.
For hope does still, encourage a will
To blossom bold and bright.

Forget Me Not

The Waxing Moon phase is perfect for instilling the intention of growing memories—be they long lost, loved and lost, or any other type in between. Hold some rosemary, rose quartz, or lovely forget-me-nots if you can, to encourage a stronger charm, and say quietly or aloud:

Spell

The sweetness of your scent is near. I wake—it's just a dream.
For life, that time, was so sublime, whenever you were near.
I think of you most every day, and hope you do the same.
A wish, I pray, please, just this day, remember me again.

Wishes Come True Ritual

You can always wish upon a star, but inviting the Moon in can help wishes come true faster! Say quietly or aloud:

Spell

Whether Moon, or star, or rainbow be—the pot of gold is there for me.
I wish I may, I wish I might, find my wish come true before the night
Doth curl its head upon the bough and sing sweet lullaby—rest now.

Boosting Success

A little success can put you over the Moon. But if it's a boost you need, speak to her—she is sure to listen. Say quietly or aloud:

Spell

Fortune, fame, accomplishment; victory, profit, thrive.
Happy, healthy, prosperous; win, prevail, arrive.
Advancing Moon, instill in me success as you define.

New Adventure

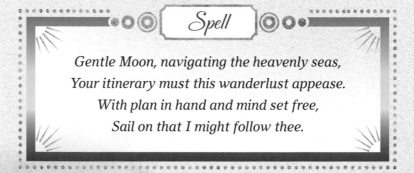

Feeling the need to spread your wings or satisfy that need for adventure? Open your heart to the Moon's inspiration to set you on your way. Say quietly or aloud:

Spell

Gentle Moon, navigating the heavenly seas,
Your itinerary must this wanderlust appease.
With plan in hand and mind set free,
Sail on that I might follow thee.

Bringing Peacefulness

Peacefulness is a tall order, but this simple spell can be useful both in raising positive vibrations around you and also in sending them out into the world, if you desire. Use the Waxing Moon to set your intentions for peaceful living, and then recite the following, quietly or aloud:

Spell

Waxing Moon, your growing light shines bright from up above,
Raising hopes, instilling dreams of peaceful times to come.
Direct your gaze, with healing love, on all who see you now,
That light may spark a single heart to action as a dove.

Take a moment to thank the Moon for her help and be grateful for peace as it is.

Fertile Blessings

If the pitter-patter of little feet beckons you, the Moon Goddess is surely on your side. For this spell, you may also wish to enlist the help of some of the goddesses worshipped for their fertility prowess—Isis, Freya, Arianrhod, and Diana, to name a few.

Gather the tools you want to work with that represent fertility to you, such as myrtle, moonstone, and perhaps a candle, and create an altar under the Waxing Moon. Take a moment to feel the Moon's growing light fill you with the energies you need to grow and tend a new life. Focus on your intentions. When you are ready, say quietly or aloud:

Spell

I stand here now, emotions high, with grateful outstretched arms–
May fruitful be my wish to thee, that pregnant do I grow.
My hopes and fears, I offer here, the rest I cannot know.
O' Goddess Moon–be boy or girl–please ply your magic charms.

Intuition Boost

The Waxing Moon's vibrational energy can heighten your natural intuition. Whether your intuition needs a boost from a slump or you need reassurance that you can trust what your intuition is telling you, try this spell.

Standing or sitting quietly, close your eyes. Let your mind be still, and listen to what your heart is telling you. Unsure what that is? Say quietly or aloud:

Spell

Cleansing Moon, cast your light—dispense the shadows nigh.
I call on you to heed my cry, awaken sights within.
Power my internal eye, make clear what I deny.

Harnessing the Power of Tiger's Eye

Tiger's eye, aptly named, is reputed to give one the ability to see, observe, sense, and bring differing views into a harmonious picture–another set of eyes on the problem. It releases fear and anxiety, instills the confidence needed to act, and provides the will to follow through. Tiger's eye energies align naturally with the Moon's Waxing Gibbous phase, when energy and excitement build and a little clarity can offer another perspective. Capricorns, with their intense productivity inclination, may find this stone useful.

Hold a tiger's eye and say quietly or aloud:

Spell

Bright and shining tiger's eye, lend me your power
To see around corners and know it's the hour
When planning and action do meet and require
Great courage and wisdom to fulfill desire.

Some People Have All the Luck

Try this simple spell during one of the Moon's waxing phases, when energy and excitement are building and have the power to spur you on.

Gather a gold or an orange candle and some matches. Sit comfortably in sight of the Moon. Place the candle on a heatproof surface and light it. Take a moment to let its light fill you with optimism as you release any negative thoughts. Say quietly or aloud:

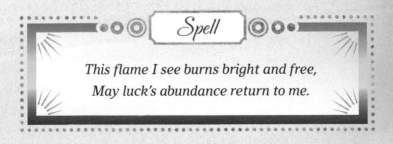

Spell

*This flame I see burns bright and free,
May luck's abundance return to me.*

Extinguish the candle and take a moment to acknowledge all in your life you are lucky for.

Getting Creative!

The Waxing phase of the Moon is your time for creative action. You've set your intentions and started the process, so don't let anything get in the way of you fulfilling your desires. Now is the time to pump up your energy and let your creative spirit fly. Opal, ylang-ylang, and the color yellow are all potential boosters for the ideas and imagination you seek.

1. Remind yourself of the intentions you've set.

2. Place any crystals, herbs, oils, or other tools you'd like on your altar. Sit quietly, focus your attention on their beauty (scent, color, shape, whatever you see), and let your thoughts flow freely.

3. Which thoughts inspire action? Which inspire new ideas? Which inspire more thought? Write these down in your journal for further meditation work.

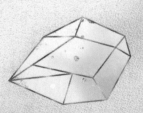

4. When you are ready, say quietly or aloud:

Spell

Moon's bright light holds rainbow hues,
an endless well of changing views.
The shapes and shadows cast about
are ever-changing signs, no doubt,
That life does shift and life does show,
For new ideas to bloom and grow,
must first begin with faith and you—
To sow, to feed, to act, to reap,
no time to waste—just take the leap.
The Moon will light the way.

Summoning Courage to Take Action

The Moon's Waxing phase is the time to take action–and sometimes that requires a bit more courage than we have.

You've been planting, nurturing, and growing the seeds of your intentions. With their imminent bloom, you may be wondering whether you've been putting your energies toward the right task. Trust your instincts and the illuminating Moon to help you see things through to their natural outcome. For a bit of extra courage, cast this simple spell. Fennel, thyme, basil, and aquamarine are all tools you can work with, if you like.

Under the light of the Waxing Moon, stand peacefully, and grateful for the chance to receive the Moon's gifts. Focus on the intention you've set or the questions you have.

When you are ready, say quietly or aloud:

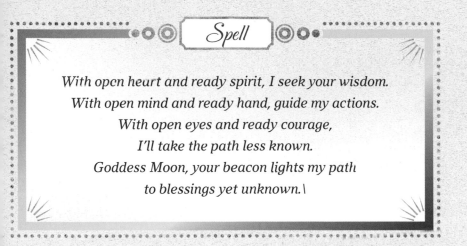

Spell

With open heart and ready spirit, I seek your wisdom.
With open mind and ready hand, guide my actions.
With open eyes and ready courage,
I'll take the path less known.
Goddess Moon, your beacon lights my path
to blessings yet unknown.

Take a moment to breathe in the light and fill your inner well with courage and confidence.

Moonlit Grounding

Grounding is the act of placing your bare feet on a natural surface–sand, soil, grass, or mud–to create a connection between your body and the earth's energy or natural charge. This can be particularly powerful during the Waxing Moon.

1. Find a peaceful place outside where the Moon is visible with a surface that is easy on your feet.

2. Stand with your bare feet on the earth. Close your eyes and breathe slowly. Wiggle your toes and shift your weight until your feet settle into a deep and comfortable connection with the ground.

3. Stay in this position for 5 minutes. Think about any challenges or obstacles you've been facing.

4. Open your eyes and slowly walk barefoot in a large circle. Take your steps gently, but with intention. Notice the way each bare foot connects with the earth. Notice your posture.

5. Walk this way for a few minutes. Revisit the questions above. You may find that you feel charged by the earth and have increased clarity when connecting with yourself, identifying the action you want to take, or addressing the challenges you may be facing.

Channeling Healing Energy

The law of vibration tells us everything vibrates. And because everything in the Universe is made differently, it vibrates at a different frequency. Some of those frequencies are obvious (like sunlight or music), but some are not. What is obvious, though, is that these energies are all interconnected and influenced by each other, much like ripples in a pond.

This simple ritual can send positive energy and vibrations anywhere they're needed.

When something happens that particularly touches you–anywhere in the world–find time to sit quietly, light a candle and visualize your good and healing intentions being manifested. Pray for pain to be eased or light to be given. Let the candle burn. Extinguish it. Give thanks to the Universe for your place in it.

Goddess Meditation Ritual

When your inner Moon goddess feels like she could use a goddess best friend this simple ritual can help you appeal to the ancient Moon goddesses who came before you. Their wisdom and power are available to get you back on track or boost your confidence so you can achieve that intention you recently set.

As each goddess can awaken different sacred feminine aspects within, ask for all their gifts or ask for a specific one depending on the intentions you've set.

Sit in meditation (you can also do this while Moon bathing) and concentrate on the goddess you wish to invite in and any specific area you wish to work on with her. For example, invite Isis to boost your confidence and the intuition you need to tackle a specific situation. When meditating, connect with the goddesses in whatever way resonates with you.

There's nothing more to it than inviting them in and sitting quietly in meditation. Pay attention to your intuitive senses: clairaudience (clear healing), clairsentience (clear feeling), claircognizance (clear knowing), and clairvoyance (clear seeing). Depending on which sense is strongest, you may hear, feel, know, or see their guidance, presence, and love.

No matter what, trust that by simply asking for their goddess support, you open yourself to connect with your divine feminine gifts, which reveal themselves subtly and mysteriously.

Speaking Your Truth

When the light of the Moon begins to show, it's time to come out of the darkness and into Mother Moon's renewing energy. Though time has moved forward, the past can linger, inhibit our aspirations, or rattle our confidence. You may believe that your intuition is off, you're not deserving of the things you want, or you're not magical anymore. No matter how you're feeling, speak with the confidence that your desires will come true. For this ritual, you will speak to Mother Moon directly.

On a night during the Crescent Moon, place a moonstone or silver item in your pocket or somewhere on your person—anywhere easily reachable. Go outside to a quiet and safe place where you and Mother Moon can be alone. As you journey to this place, palm your charm, repeating your truth in your head.

Finally, when you're alone, take 5 deep breaths. Imagine any doubt or fear blowing out with each exhale and the Moon's energy coming in with each inhale. Look up at the Moon and say:

Spell

Mother Moon, bringer of light
Who gives me guidance in the night,
Protect me and help me with my dream.
Show me it's not as scary as it may seem.
Give me the courage to speak my truth
Help me trust in me as I trust in you.

Feel the words burn in your chest and then on your tongue. Then, as if it is reality, speak your magic into existence. Say it loud and proud. Don't shrink back or doubt your ability. Thank the Moon for her time and for her blessing.

Loose-Leaf Clarity Journal

The Waxing Moon Crescent Moon is about fine-tuning and clarifying your plans and intentions. It'll take some contemplation and a lot of creativity.

What you'll need:

- ◆ Loose-leaf journal pages
- ◆ Paints
- ◆ Brushes
- ◆ Scissors
- ◆ Glue
- ◆ Pictures
- ◆ Pens
- ◆ Colored pencils
- ◆ Stickers
- ◆ Stencils
- ◆ Alfalfa for manifestation
- ◆ Peony for success
- ◆ Jasmine for clarity
- ◆ Orange candle for creativity (optional)
- ◆ Yellow candle for manifestation (optional)
- ◆ Yellow ribbon (optional)
- ◆ Yellow envelope (optional)

Before fully jumping in, write your goal in big letters and clear, succinct language on a piece of loose-leaf paper. Tie, staple, or glue a small piece of alfalfa to it for manifestation. Alfalfa is a powerful plant that elevates the energy of whatever spell it's attached to. Follow a similar pattern for each page.

With each page, be as colorful, loud, and imaginative as possible. As you're creating your pages, be sure to include jasmine or peony (whether a drawing, picture, herb, or petal) on each page to give it an extra kick. You can also burn some candles and let the wax drip onto the pages.

When you're done, tie the pages together with the ribbon, contain them in an envelope, or even display them around your room or altar. Do what feels right to you.

Tiny Money Bundle Charm

Money, money, money. Some say the love of it is the root of all evil. Although greed is definitely an undesirable quality, the reality is that everyone needs money. In many ways, everything in our modern-day lives is governed by money– we need it to live, enjoy life, and feel secure. The Waxing Crescent phase of the Moon is the perfect time to start attracting money to carry you through the rest of the month and beyond.

This tiny bundle will act as your money-attracting charm to help extra funds come your way when you need them most.

What you'll need:

♦ A tiny Wheel of Fortune tarot card
   (it can be a printed-out version)
♦ Bay leaf for success
♦ Green thread or ribbon to represent luck
♦ A form of currency to use as a money charm

Perform this spell on a Sunday, as it's a day of wealth and prosperity. Try to time your spell so it occurs sometime between 12 p.m. and 2 p.m., when the Sun is at his peak. Next, clean out your wallet. This means taking every card, receipt, or paper clutter that's taking up unnecessary space. Sprinkle sea salt over your wallet to cleanse it from the previous energies. Now, place all the important things, such as your identification and credit cards, back in, but leave room for the bundle.

Arrange your bundle with the Wheel of Fortune card first. This card represents abundance but ultimately also balance. No matter what happens in life, everything eventually lands in its place. Next, use the bay leaf and consecrated pen to write out your wish for attracting money, or draw the Fehu rune for success and money on the leaf.

Last, pick a money charm that's special to you. It can be a crisp dollar bill, a gold coin representing new wealth, or maybe a $2 bill for luck. Once everything's ready, tie the bundle together with the green thread and tuck it into your wallet.

Honing Your
Psychic Abilities

Potential lies in the First Quarter Moon. It's the time to take action and learn a new skill. Psychic and divination magic sound mysterious, almost like there's a cloud closing it off from those who don't have the natural gift. But that's far from the truth! Whether you have innate abilities or not, anyone can benefit from the First Quarter Moon's power to help you develop a new skill and get in tune with a new realm.

There are roughly six types of psychics: automatic writers and drawers, clairvoyants, psychokinetics, precognition witches, psychometrics, and remote viewing witches. If you've never explored this side of witchcraft, you may not know which type you are. This ritual will help you connect with Spirit, and you'll discover where your talents lie.

What you'll need:

◆ Cornflower to enhance psychic abilities
◆ Goldenrod to awaken your ability to sense emotions, vibrations, and energies
◆ Mint to strengthen divination and help communication with Spirit
◆ Lemongrass oil for receiving messages from Spirit
◆ A purple candle to open your third eye
◆ A silver candle to represent the Moon
◆ Purple altar cloth

Set up your altar with the purple cloth and scatter the herbs along the fabric. No need to change them in any way; their presence alone is meant to aid you. Light both candles, and when you're settled, take several deep breaths. Try to slow your breath as much as possible to enter into a meditative state.

Now, imagine an antenna going up from the crown of your head and say:

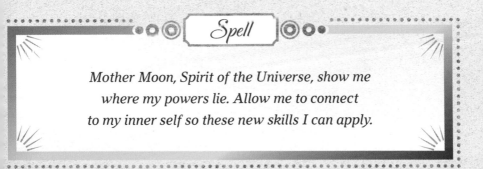

Mother Moon, Spirit of the Universe, show me where my powers lie. Allow me to connect to my inner self so these new skills I can apply.

Listen closely to the message you receive. When you get your answer, give thanks and rejoice.

Jupiter, Planet of Luck

The First Quarter of the Moon is a time to experiment with different ways of manifesting your desires. It's an ideal time to try your luck spells. As the Moon grows brighter and more powerful, so can your magic. For this spell, you'll call upon the power of Jupiter, the planet of luck. Its massive size and gravitational pull have garnered it eighty known Moons, including the Galilean Moons Io, Europa, Callisto, and Ganymede, the largest in our solar system.

Jupiter paired with the First Quarter Moon will aid you in whatever luck you seek for yourself.

What you'll need:

♦ A green candle for prosperity
♦ An orange candle for success
♦ Agate for manifestation
♦ Citrine for luck
♦ Tiger's eye for abundance
♦ A green piece of clothing, string, or patch to wear

Perform the spell on a Thursday, as it's the day for luck. To begin, carve the sign for Jupiter on the orange candle. On the green candle, write the area in your life in which you want luck. Light both candles. Next, collect the crystals in your hands and hold them tightly but comfortably. Focus on your desire and then imagine what life would look like if you got the luck you want. Keep that image in your mind and meditate on it until you can see a clear picture.

When the image is its clearest, say aloud:

Spell

O' Jupiter, planet of fortune, show me the sagaciousness of success. Remind me that attainment is my sacred right and prosperity will always be in my line of sight.

Drop the crystals onto the altar as a way of releasing your energy into the world. Let both candles burn out before cleaning your altar.

Nightstand Dream Altar

The Waxing Gibbous Moon phase is the part of the month when the Moon is on the cusp of becoming whole. It's a time of increased power, yet also a time of observation. This is a good time to observe your dreams. Because dreams are so powerful and mysterious, we should dabble in dream magic at least once! Feel free to adjust this spell to fit the specific dreams you want to have or the type of dream magic you want.

What you'll need:

♦ Black altar cloth for protection
♦ Clear quartz for communicating with Spirit
♦ Amethyst for opening your third-eye chakra
♦ A black candle for banishing any nightmares
♦ 3 juniper berries for dream travel
♦ The Priestess tarot card to represent your dream guide

Clear your nightstand of any clutter. You'll want your altar to be solely focused on dreaming. Clean the surface with cleansing salt, incense, or a cleansing spray. Place the black cloth down, arrange the crystals, and then place the candle. Arrange the juniper berries in a triangle around the candle to represent you, Spirit, and your dream state. Lastly, have The Priestess card face you so she can watch over you as you travel into a dream state. With this by your bedside, your dreams are about to become a lot more interesting.

Anti-Anxiety Adventure Sachet

With everything going on in life, coping with anxiety can be a challenge. Mother Moon can help alleviate this stress, but sometimes we're in our own way.

The time of the Waxing Gibbous Moon is one for nurturing your life, feeding your soul, and recognizing what binds you. This spell will put you in the mindset of releasing anxiety and allowing yourself to go, have fun, and make some memories.

Grab your journal and set your intention. What kind of adventure do you want to have? Identify what's stopping you from taking the plunge. Is it that you're afraid of the world out there? Why don't you feel ready? Sit with your patron deity and ask them for courage and strength to continue on your path.

For the next 9 days (the number for courage), add one herb a day to your sachet. Use a yellow bag for your sachet, because yellow represents manifestation, confidence, and success.

Use this order to add herbs to your sachet:

1. Daisy for your intention

2. Allspice for courage

3. Ginger for dealing with emotional stress

4. Thyme for confidence in yourself

5. Fennel for the strength to be who you truly are, and that's an adventurer

6. Dandelion for resiliency

7. Nutmeg for purpose

8. Parsley for momentum

9. Cinnamon for energizing power

At the end of the nine days, take your sachet with you when you're ready. Thank the Moon for her help.

Full Moon Spells

THE MOON REACHING HER FULL phase is the equivalent to her reaching womanhood. She's gone through her stages of growth, she's put actions behind her words, and now she's here to celebrate. It has taken a lot of movement and momentum for her to get to where she is, as it has for those who follow her. The Full Moon phase is multifaceted. It's a time of celebration, gratitude, and blessings, but it's also a time in which anything can happen. Any spell you want to do will have the most power during this time.

You've been through a time of learning, of new beginnings, and of adventures, and now you've reached your peak. The Full Moon is a special time during the Moon's cycle because it's a period of celebration. The Moon has finally matured into Mother Moon, meaning she's rife with blessings and vigor. She can not only shine her brightest, but she can pass her strength to us. It's a time of abundance, celebration, joy, and gratitude.

In this phase, the Moon represents summer, when there's nothing but light, fun, activities, bounties of all kinds, and happiness. It's here that she brings about manifestation. All the work you put in up until this point has come or is about to come to fruition. Mother Moon has an air of wild energy about her.

Her excitement and peak energy are perfect for influencing us to think outside the box, whether in our personal life or in spellwork. You can perform virtually any spell during this time, and it will be its most potent. Whether you want to make Moon water, consecrate your tools, or find what you've lost, this is when you harness the wonderfully erratic might of the Moon.

Moon Water

During the Moon's Full phase, when her energy is at its height, place a large lidded container outside (in your yard or on a balcony or porch) where it can catch the Moon's beams, or place it near a window that receives Moonlight. Fill it with water (use spring or distilled water if you'll be using it for culinary purposes), cover the container, and let it bathe in the light of the Moon. Take a moment to focus your intentions into the water, and then let it infuse with the Moon's nourishing energy.

The next day, the water will be ready to use. Label it and keep refrigerated, if you wish. Add the water to your Moon bath, use it to brew Moon Tea, immerse your crystals in it to reenergize them, or just sip it as you meditate in the Moon's guiding light.

Moon Dancing

With all that great energy emanating from the Full Moon (the original disco ball in the sky!), now's the time for a dance party. Invite the neighbors or your friends for a formalized group event, or keep it simple with just you. Crank up the tunes–let your inner rhythms guide you–and dance to celebrate life and the culmination of another month's work.

Feel the energy cleanse your soul and the joy fill your heart. When finished, take a moment to be quiet and give thanks.

The Full Moon
and Your Birth Month

If you'd like to incorporate a ritual or two to mark the occasion of your birthday, consider a Moon bath or create a Moon circle. Although the Full Moon represents a culmination of sorts, it's also a time to give thanks and be grateful for who we are and all we have.

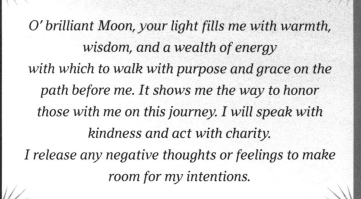

Spell

O' brilliant Moon, your light fills me with warmth, wisdom, and a wealth of energy with which to walk with purpose and grace on the path before me. It shows me the way to honor those with me on this journey. I will speak with kindness and act with charity.
I release any negative thoughts or feelings to make room for my intentions.

Energy Boost for Your Favorite Sports Team

Gather a clear quartz (recently charged by a Full Moon, if possible) for maximum energy and an object representing your team (such as a jersey, hat, photo, or the like). Place the crystal on the object and take a minute to connect your energies with the crystal. When you are ready, say quietly or aloud:

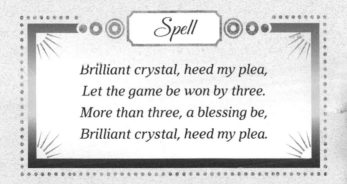

Spell

Brilliant crystal, heed my plea,
Let the game be won by three.
More than three, a blessing be,
Brilliant crystal, heed my plea.

Repeat three times. Take a moment to visualize a celebration and thank the crystal for its work.

Good Luck

Dill and the color green are thought to bring luck. Using the energy of a Full Moon offers the help of gravity's pull at its strongest to absorb the power of good luck. Use this simple spell when you feel the need for a boost in the luck category. Gather some dill seeds, a large clay pot, some potting soil, gravel, and water. Take everything outside and stand in the Moon's light (a Full Moon has the most energy potential). Focus your thoughts on the area in which you'd like a lucky strike to occur. Be specific and imagine it happening.

Add a bit of gravel to the pot for drainage. Fill the pot with soil and sprinkle the seeds over the soil. Cover with a light dusting of soil to keep them in place. As you water the seeds, say quietly or aloud:

Spell

Magnificent Moon, I ask your energy to warm these seeds that my luck may grow as abundantly and fearlessly as they. Thank you for your nurturing light.

Place the pot in a warm area where it will receive sunlight–in addition to Moonlight–and the seeds should sprout in about ten days. Check on the seeds periodically and water when the dirt is dry. Feel your luck grow as the dill stems grow ever higher. Use the fresh herbs for any number of dishes, from soups to pickles to potato salad and salmon. Sprinkle some luck into your everyday meals!

Conjuring Clarity

The Full Moon is a time for seeing fully and clearly. If you're feeling a bit muddle-headed and just need some help shaking out the cobwebs, try this spell:

Spell

In Full Moon I stand, seeking a hand,
to wipe the fog from my eyes.
So clearly I see what matters to me
and actions to meet, thus required.
Full Moon, take my hand–help me understand,
to realize my dreams and desires.

Giving Thanks

The Full Moon fills us to the brim. Take a moment to give thanks and a nod of gratitude for the bounty in your life—and then pass it on. Say quietly or aloud:

Spell

I thank you, Moon, for all you do to guide and comfort me.
I thank you, friends, for all you give—your love, support, and glee.
And so I stand beneath your light with a heart so full of love,
To know my life is blessed, you see, without you I have none.

Fair Weather

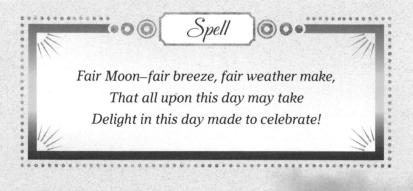

Whether for a wedding, travel, a sports event, or a day off, beautiful weather is always welcome. Check in with the Full Moon for some help with the forecast. Say quietly or aloud:

Spell

Fair Moon—fair breeze, fair weather make,
That all upon this day may take
Delight in this day made to celebrate!

Feeling Powerful Ritual

Can you feel the power? No? Well, turn to the powerful Full Moon for a boost of energy so you can have what it takes. Say quietly or aloud:

Spell

There's power in numbers, but this time just one.
Full Moon, help me gather the courage that I need,
To show them the power is, yes, mine indeed!

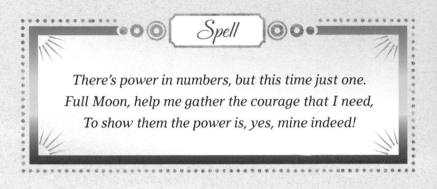

Finding Something Lost

Think of the Full Moon as a supercharged flashlight whose gravitational pull can help pull you toward that item you've misplaced. Try it!

Spell

Tides of Nature heed your cry, and swiftly they obey.
Cast your beaming rays this way to help me with this plea,
For lost again, this thing I need is set not in its place,
Return to me, Moon's gravity, what's lost in time and space.

Clear Quartz Clarity Ritual

Clear quartz crystals are extremely powerful, meaning they can take on whatever you've got to offer. Their powerful energies are particularly useful during a Full Moon. Be specific in your intentions when working with clear quartz and they'll absorb them fully. Be sure to listen to the energy vibes they send out in return. In a nod to its all-purpose nature, this crystal can be helpful to all signs of the Zodiac to amplify intentions, counteract negative energy, and find acceptance. It is also the crystal of wisdom.

When choices abound and decisions elude, seek clear quartz's power. Holding the crystal and feeling its warmth and energy, unite with the Moon's energy to amplify your focus. Say quietly or aloud:

Spell

In times like these I know I must decide what's right and true.
Pray, Moon, you might, with crystal's sight, help guide me as I choose.
In stillness here I listen now. I wait to hear my muse.

Allspice Herbal Magic

The properties and fragrance of compassionate allspice are energizing and uplifting, and it works nicely in restorative spells. Allspice's magical worth includes attracting fortune and luck in the business arena, and it's beneficial in any combination to invoke healing.

Used in a tea, allspice can soothe digestive upset. Used in a bath in essential oil form, it can ease aching muscles. Place allspice berries in a sachet and carry in your purse or wallet to attract money and luck. When used as a culinary seasoning, it can improve the diner's mood and enhance feelings of positivity.

Bury some allspice berries, under the light of the Full Moon, in your garden, in a pot, or in clean soil in a dish on your altar. Come back the next day and say quietly or aloud to the charged berries:

Spell

Allspice, all good, all wishes are buried with you.
Unleash your rich fragrance into the world
that my world becomes richer for it.

Moonflower
Herbal Magic Spell

Moonflower has a nocturnal nature that means revealing dreams of love. Enchanting white flowers open in late afternoon, as darkness hovers and the Moon begins to show, and stay open for one night only. Note: This plant is poisonous and is best incorporated into an herbal Moon garden for inviting pollinators and encouraging the magical growth cycle. As a flower ruled by the Moon, moonflower is a must for any herbal Moon garden, so it can be used in Moon spells and for divination, dreams, and intuition.

Under the light of the Full Moon, inhale moonflower's perfume to induce prophetic dreams and awaken your intuition.

Spell

*For herbs at this hour have magic and
power beyond when the Sun's in the sky.
In darkness you see, reveal unto me,
your prophecy, truth, and desire.*

Summoning
the Goddesses of Wisdom
and Knowledge

These are goddesses whose powers reign supreme and whose
knowledge is vast and varied, representing the original
STEAM (science, technology, engineering, arts, and math–or
magic!) team. They can heal, nurture, guide, protect, teach,
and help you survive. When life brings you to a crossroads,
you'll have help deciding which path to take.

They know herbs, magic, and medicine. Their realms are of
books, buildings, and civilizations. Their energies are less
emotional and more factual. They honor past, present, and
future. You'll even find some lessons in manners along the
way. When working with these goddesses, bathe in their
healing waters, listen to their wise counsel, and learn from
their mistakes.

Give thanks for the time, trouble, and ill fortune they may save you, and give back by spreading your knowledge far and wide to help others manifest their dreams. Above all, recognize the talents of those who came before you, give thanks, and lift up others with your wisdom so that their knowledge and wisdom may shine bright into the future.

Spell

*With goddess sense of sight so keen
the darkness turns to light,
You're stirred to spread your wings aloft
with Full Moon shining bright.
Your wisdom comes with strength
to know when telling will delight,
Or guiding breeze needs whisper
sweet soft words of true and right.
O' brilliant one who soars so deft
that not a sound is made,
Do help me see beyond the trees
when guiding light does fade.*

Deep Healing Ritual

Feeling the full weight of the Moon's energy, breathe deeply to fill your body from head to toe with her warmth. Reflect on what needs to be healed and create a picture in your mind of what that looks like. Keeping the picture in focus, when you are ready, say one or both of these spells quietly or aloud:

Spell

Goddess Moon, tend to me in this time of ill.
May your light mend my heart and help my mind be still.
Bring me peace that I may use my energy to heal.
Goddess Moon, shine on me that better I may feel.

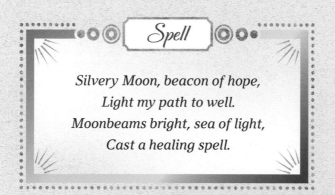

Spell

Silvery Moon, beacon of hope,
Light my path to well.
Moonbeams bright, sea of light,
Cast a healing spell.

Sacred Moon Circle

Your circle is your sacred space. It can be made with physical objects, such as crystals or stones, or it can simply be drawn with your finger in the air. It is a place to gather and a place to create energy. It is a powerful place.

Gather your friends under the next Full Moon. Connect and amplify their energies by joining hands in a circle, standing or sitting, possibly around an altar you've made. If desired, each person can place an object to be charged with the Moon's energy inside the circle or on the altar. The purpose of your circle is to celebrate and honor the Goddess Moon and all her gifts and to open yourself to her light, increasing intuition.

Use the circle for intention setting. Create and chant your own mantra to raise the energies around you. Stand or sit silently and meditate on your intentions. Sing or dance clockwise in the circle. Light a candle in memory of someone or something when it's time to bring the circle to a close. Take a moment to give thanks for the seasonal blessings of the Moon and friends. Walk or dance counterclockwise to dissolve the circle.

Blessed be.

Money Moon Ritual

Take advantage of the unique power of a Blue Moon to fill yourself with energy and purpose or to refocus.

Go outside and breathe in the light and energy of the Moon. Having a green jade stone with you will boost your lucky energies and bring opportunities for wealth.

Keep a clear head and focus on the problem to be solved. What will help? For example, could you polish the resume, apply for a new job, approach your boss about a raise, or set a budget and keep to it?

What will you do to increase your worth, not just monetarily, this month?

Spell

When gentle waves of Moonbeams sing,
soft charming songs doth tell,
Of shimmering riches, lo' behold,
there borne upon their wings.

Blue Moon Ritual

Take advantage of the beauty and light this special Full Moon offers by performing a ritual for focusing your thoughts. It can be as simple or elaborate as you like.

Clear your space of negative energy and thought; a simple way is to tidy the space and spray a favorite scent, diffuse an essential oil, or anything else that gives you a feeling of freshness.

Light a candle to set the mood; its color or scent may depend on what desires you want to be fulfilled. Or, use white or blue to mirror the Blue Moon's silent energy.

Sit comfortably somewhere, outside or in, you can see the Moon's glow. Close your eyes or gaze into the candle flame. Breathe deeply, feeling the Moon's pull with each breath in and releasing any tension or negative thoughts with each breath out.

Concentrate on your intention. Do you want to fill your life with more joy? Do you want to boost self-esteem so you are ready to tackle the world? Whatever it is, when you're ready, say quietly or aloud:

Spell

I am filled with the Moon's guiding light.
I am filled with joy.
In this light, I see I am strong;
I feel safe and loved.
I can live joyfully,
and I will live purposefully
to care for myself and others.
Thank you for your energy
and wisdom, fair Moon.

Let the candle burn down. Take time to reflect on your thoughts or write them in your journal.

Lunar Eclipse Magic: Moon Wishes

Because lunar eclipses occur during Full Moons, they offer a special time to honor change, celebrate growth and healing, and tap into our inner resolve. If you can, stand outside and feel the energy of aligning with the Universe: Sun, Earth, you, and the Moon, all in harmony. Consider a ritual to honor the event and give thanks to the power of Nature to heal. Mark the occasion alone or invite your favorite group of like-minded friends.

1. Pick a location where the Moon is visible. In good weather, being outdoors lets you feel that full connection with Nature and its calming, harmonious influence.

2. Cleanse the space with a sage smudge or incense.

3. Set an altar, if desired, with special objects, crystals, or other natural items.

4. Set the mood: music, candles, comfortable places to sit, and food (and wine) are all great options.

5. Gather paper, pens, and matches (if you need to let go of something), as well as a proper container in which to burn something.

6. Take time to meditate on your intentions and then write them down. Writing down our goals increases our rate of success in achieving them. Share them with the group, if you like. Stating intentions aloud, to others, helps cement our accountability to them.

7. Put your Moon wishes in a special place–under your pillow, in a wish box, or in an intention jar, for example–and observe the results.

Moon Bathing
for Purification

In addition to cleansing our bodies, cleansing our psyches is an important part of self-care. Moon bathing is a simple yet relaxing, soul-cleansing, and mind-clearing ritual that useful at any phase of the Moon, but it is said to be most powerful during a Full Moon, when the Moon's purifying energy is at its highest.

Moonlight or water? You do what you prefer and what feels comfortable. If you're lucky enough to live in a warmer climate year-round, bathing in the Moon's light outside, feeling truly connected to the Earth below your feet and the wondrous stars above, can bring an immense sense of peace. If your luck runs higher and you live near a body of water, a dip in the ocean, river, or lake (even the pool!), can be enormously healing and fulfilling. For everyone else, take advantage of those warmer evenings in summer and fall. No natural water? Use the nearest tub.

Moon Bath Ritual
by Moonlight

Prepare a spot in your yard or a park, on a porch, on a balcony, or even near a window, any darkened place you feel safe, connected to Nature, and able to touch the Moon's light will work. Create an altar or offering nearby, if desired, using favorite items such as crystals, candles, incense, photos, or other special objects that relate to your intentions that month and that you'd like to cleanse with the Moon's energy. (Be sure to bring proper holders for any burning objects, along with water and/or a fire extinguisher when you are using flames outdoors.)

Comfortably stand or sit under the Moon's most powerful light, close your eyes, and feel your hands (if sitting) and feet firmly planted to the ground. Breathe. Deeply in. Slowly out. Again. Focus your thoughts on filling your body with the Moon's light and energy with every breath in. With every breath out, feel the energy of your breath and assess the results of your actions this past month. What new insights do they reveal?

Moon Bath Ritual in the Bathtub

Immersing yourself in water during the Full Moon is another way to feel the pull of the Moon's heightened energy.

Create your magical space, whether with light, music, a journal, or the like, and fill your tub with warm water. Add any salts (such as Himalayan), essential oils, flowers (such as rose petals), or herbs (such as lavender) you like. Around or in the bath, arrange some water-friendly crystals such as rose quartz for unconditional love, compassion, and peace, clear quartz for power, seed crystal for wisdom, moonstone, for connecting to your inner goddess, or amethyst for protection to tap into their individual energies.

Step into the tub, immerse yourself, close your eyes, and relax. Feel the water's gentle warmth and softness cradling you, and imagine the energy it absorbs from the Moon filling you.

Let yourself feel the flow of energy throughout your body. Stay as long as is comfortable. Gently retune to the world around you when you are finished.

Celebrate the Cosmos

The Full Moon represents a time of actualization. Whether it has taken one Moon cycle or three, your prayers, wishes, and dreams are coming to fruition. With this uptick in your life, you may be feeling not only gratitude for the Moon but for the cosmos as a whole. If you're feeling strong gratitude for the good in your life, perform this ritual.

Go outside on a night during the Full Moon while wearing silver to honor the Moon. Bring something that represents the other planets, such as an astrology chart. When you're alone and safe, say a prayer for each planet, for its purpose, and for what it represents to you. Thank the planets for their effects and energies, for what they've given you so far, and for what they will give you in the future. Sing to them if that's what you want, or you can perform the Moon Dance or do anything else that communicates your thanks.

Afterward, take in the Moon's light and let it wash over you.

High Vibration Happiness

During this special time, the Full Moon signals that the Moon's power is at its highest, meaning it's also the time for peak energy output. That includes high-energy emotions such as love, fear, anger, and, the most powerful of all, happiness.

Whether you need to get in the right mindset for your spellwork or you want to be most powerful, this spell will have you zinging with happy vibrations to strengthen your practice.

What you'll need:

♦ Your favorite article of clothing or accessory
♦ Good music for dancing or singing to
♦ Your favorite scent (body spray, candle incense, etc.)
♦ Any pictures that bring positive memories
♦ Peppermint essential oil that's safe for consumption for uplifting energy
♦ Yellow candle for joy (you can also include more colors you have a positive association with)
♦ Celestine to raise vibrations

The goal is to create the happiest and most pleasant atmosphere you can. Cast a magic circle to keep bad influences out and, more importantly, to keep the good in. You're going to become a spiritual firecracker, all light and power, so you'll want to keep it concentrated.

Put on your favorite article of clothing and take a moment to let its comfort seep into you. Next, add your favorite scents. Arrange your altar with the candles and pictures. Put a drop or two of the essential oil right on your tongue. Then, hold the celestine in your hand, turn on the music, and do as your heart delights. Dance, sing, laugh, reminisce–anything that brings you happiness! Feel the crystal vibrate in your hand, and become one with it.

As you collect joy, imagine your happiness as a firework being lit and then hurtling toward the sky and exploding in a rush of color. Keep the energy going for as long as you can. Then, when you're on the comedown, thank Mother Moon for her part in your happiness.

This spell can be paired with other spells to increase energy.

Moon Water Beauty

Beauty isn't solely about outward appearances. Oftentimes, beauty comes from within. Even so, because of social media, the prevalence of over-edited photos, and television, it can be challenging to recognize your unique beauty. That's when the Full Moon and her energy come in. Not only will her light shine on you physically, it will come through emotionally.

This Moon water spell is intended to make you feel as though you're at a lovely spa, but also to boost your confidence and your aura. If you're having a hard time with self-esteem, this spell is perfect for you.

What you'll need:

- Full Moon water (do not use distilled water)
- Pink salt to cleanse your aura
- Orange peel (can be dried) to reveal your true beauty
- Chamomile for peace
- Lavender for impactful self-love
- Dried rose for a feeling of luxury
- Jasmine for amplification
- A mirror
- An eyedropper
- Cotton balls or rounds
- Your cauldron
- A second clean bowl

Place the herbs in your cauldron. With each ingredient, say its purpose aloud to connect with its meaning and let the words wash over you. Take your prepared Moon water and warm it up to a temperature that's pleasant to the skin. Sprinkle the herbs in the water and let sit for five minutes.

Afterward, use the eyedropper to transfer water to a cotton pad. Rub the cotton gently over your face and neck. Do this slowly, so you're able to both smell the fragrance and feel the magic taking its effect.

Once you're satisfied, look in the mirror and notice your aura. Then describe what's beautiful about it. How is it unique to you, and what do you like about it? Recite this spell:

Spell

*My beauty shines from within,
and it glows from without.
And that's all I need.*

Hypnotic Manifestation Ritual

There are moments when our dreams can seem unattainable. Negative thinking patterns come from the idea that we're asking for too much or dreaming too big. But are we? Who's to say that we can't have what we want?

The Full Moon is when you're meant to take chances and put your all behind a spell or intention. Save this ritual for a big wish because it might take a lot out of you. You can pair this ritual with a watered-down version of the High Vibration Happiness Spell (see page 108) for an extra boost.

What you'll need:

♦ Jasper for grounding
♦ A gold candle for good fortune
♦ Wordless music or earplugs
♦ A blanket or garment to make you feel safe and cocooned

Cast your magic circle, light the candle, and plug your ears with either the music or earplugs. Sit across from the gold candle and stare into the flame, watching it move and dance. Then begin to slow your breathing until you're in a relaxed, meditative state. As you stare into the flame, let the glow of it burn into your mind until you can close your eyes and still see it.

With that vision in mind, superimpose your will onto the light. Get as honest and as specific as possible. Let yourself go. As you hold this image in your mind, chant:

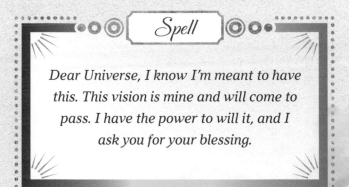

Spell

Dear Universe, I know I'm meant to have this. This vision is mine and will come to pass. I have the power to will it, and I ask you for your blessing.

Consecrating and Rededicating Ritual

Especially when first starting out, we need physical instruments to help guide our intentions and will. And just like with any tool, we use them, clean them, and then put them aside until they're needed again.

The Full Moon is a time of gratitude for our lives, for the work we've done up until this point, and for the things that have helped us on our way. It's also a time of rejuvenation and recommitment. This applies to us *and* our tools. Use this time of the month to reconsecrate and rededicate your tools to the Moon and receive all her blessings.

Go outside to meet the Moon in her space (or if you can't, go to a window facing the Full Moon). Bring your assortment of tools with you in the case or chest you usually keep them in as well as a large blanket. Find a spot wide enough that you can lay each tool out on the blanket without it being too crowded. Do so tool by tool, feeling the texture and size of every piece. Think of how each thing came into your possession. What attracted you to it? Why did you need it? How does it help you?

Once everything is laid out, look up at the Moon and her beauty. Breathe in the night air, extracting the energy from it, and hover your hands above your spices, wand, crystals, and the like. As you move, say:

Spell

Mother Moon, bless these tools
you've brought into my life.
They've served me well
in success and strife.
I claim them again as mine,
and I rededicate them
to my practice and shrine.
Thank you.

Channel your energy and that of the Moon into them so they're purified and linked to you anew.

4

Waning Moon Spells

THE WANING MOON CYCLE IS A period of rest, similar to fall and winter. Goals have been met, blessings have been bestowed, and it is time for the Moon's descent. This is called the Crone phase, when the Moon grows old and settles in before starting the cycle over again. It's during this time that everything slows down and there's room for reflection and contemplation. The Waning Moon is all about banishing the bad, readjusting after changes, and resting. This chapter will help you seek wisdom, clear a cluttered mind, and protect yourself from harmful influences.

Just like a wise woman whose life is mostly behind her, the Waning Moon looks forward, knowing things are coming to their natural close.

This lunar cycle encompasses the Waning Gibbous, Last Quarter, and Waning Crescent Moons. The Waning Gibbous Moon still has most of her power with her, but it's funneling out of her little by little. It's here that the Moon recognizes that the power she has left can be used to nurture those around her. Traditionally, the Waning Gibbous Moon is about protection, service to others, harvest, and letting go. The Moon has achieved her goals, and now she's releasing the bad and focusing solely on the good.

The Last Quarter Moon truly feels like the beginning of an end. The beauty of this phase is that we can look back on what has occurred and see it clearly. Breakdown, readjustment, and transition spells best fit this part in the Moon cycle.

During the Waning Crescent Moon, the Crone knows her work is mostly done. This is truly the end, and with finality approaching, it's best to let go of what's no longer necessary. Take this time to free yourself from anything that no longer serves you, to cleanse, and to rest. You've earned your peace.

Illuminating a Path
in Darkness

This is a particularly good ritual to adopt during the Waning Crescent Moon, as darkness sets in and you reflect on lessons learned and let go of the unproductive. It can help clear negativity from your mind and free you to act in your own best interest.

Gather a sheet of paper, a pen, a heatproof container, and matches.

Sitting quietly, use the pen and paper to write out everything you are feeling–uncensored.

Do you see any surprises or insights about recurring issues that are important to you? Have you been ignoring or suppressing your feelings in a certain area? Have you been settling, compromising, or dismissing your truth and boundaries? Are you ready to release what's no longer serving you?

You don't need to have all the answers, but it's important to ask the questions.

The paper now holds your emotions. To let go of what's bothering you, carefully burn the paper in the heatproof container while visualizing the smoke carrying the negativity into the skies. Wash away any ashes or surrender them to Mother Earth, and feel the lightness of releasing what ailed you.

Take a moment to reflect on what you learned and what you will do to move forward. Create an intention such as the following to close the ritual. When you are ready, say quietly or aloud:

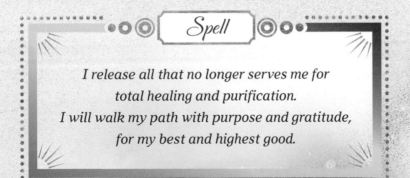

Spell

I release all that no longer serves me for
total healing and purification.
I will walk my path with purpose and gratitude,
for my best and highest good.

Conjuring Patience and Understanding

Not everyone thinks or acts as we do. But we learn so much from the differences in our world when we just take the time. For those days when you feel a bit off-kilter compared to everyone else, seek balance in the Moon's soothing glow. Say quietly or aloud:

Spell

In quiet light, I stand in peace; I listen for the words.
With quiet mind, I hear the hymn of life unfold its tune.
Of quiet heart I am, and know, you'll help me find the rhythm,
For sing us all, with different words, a song in unison.

Insight Invitation Ritual

The dark of the Waning Crescent phase is a time when things naturally slow. The Moon's energizing light is at its lowest volume. Now is the perfect time to take stock of the results of your intentions this lunar cycle and seek wisdom in solving problems still with you. Recite this spell when you need to see through the darkness and into the light of truth.

Spell

Restful Moon, whose darkness falls upon this day,
Give time to shine this light of mine on thoughts I've kept at bay.
May wisdom bloom, and truth be known
That problems fall away.

Blessing Your Resume

Maybe at the New Moon you set your intention to find a new job and now you are busy with all that requires. The Waning Moon's period of reflection is a great time to dust off the resume so it shines as brightly as you do!

Journaling about your likes, dislikes, achievements, challenges, goals, objectives, and specific areas in which you'd like to grow and improve can be great brainstorming for polishing your resume.

This can be a tough task, so before you begin, send this affirmation toward the Moon, so that she returns her light and sparkle to you:

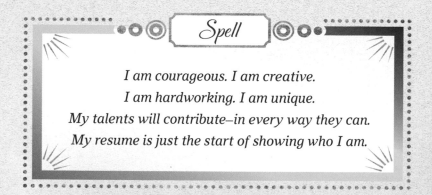

Spell

I am courageous. I am creative.
I am hardworking. I am unique.
My talents will contribute—in every way they can.
My resume is just the start of showing who I am.

Take a moment to be grateful for your uniqueness, and then get to work revising that resume.

Seeking Wisdom Ritual

There are times when just the facts are not enough. You must also have wisdom and knowledge about what to do–or not do– with the information. Understanding the hidden implications of information and messages and acting on them appropriately sometimes mean calling on a higher power.

When those moments face you, offer the following, quietly or aloud, to the wise Moon, and be open to her illuminating messages:

Spell

O' knowing Moon, I seek your help, for sagely must I see,
My head says, "Yes," my heart says, "No"–my friends, not one agrees.
With choices hard and outcomes real, please wisely advise me.

Attitude Adjustment

We all experience times when negativity begins to drag us into the mire. When a quick change of attitude is really all that's required to reverse the course of your mood, try this cheerful spell:

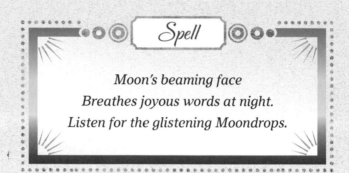

Spell

Moon's beaming face
Breathes joyous words at night.
Listen for the glistening Moondrops.

Aging Gracefully

Growing older is one of life's great joys. Don't be tempted to fight Nature's plan. When it gets you down or you start to give in to the fears, embrace the Moon's knowing grace. Say quietly or aloud:

Spell

You look the same today,
as the day that you were born.
How do you do it, Goddess Moon?
Please tell your secrets now.
My list grows long of aches, of pains,
of wrinkles and repairs, of graying hair–
I sit and stare and wonder where I've gone.
Though I may look a wee bit different
in face than that before,
I'm here, inside, with childlike eyes
that see wonder in your every turn.

Sweet Dreams Blessing

When night pulls her gentle curtain across the sky, summon the Waning Moon to tell her stories of peaceful dreams. Say quietly or aloud:

Spell

Your night's warm glow, its lovely show, does softly ease my fears.
As sleep draws nigh, I hear your tales, soft-whispered in my ears.
That dreams they bring do carry me, so gently, to that land,
Of nod and doze, in calm repose, I slumber like a bear.

Clearing a Cluttered Mind

When you just can't shake your worries loose, it's time for a bit of mental housekeeping. The Waning Moon is the time to pack up those mental troubles and let them go. Amethyst, with its soothing energies, can help. Holding the stone, take a few deep, calming breaths. Focus on the worries you'd like to release and let the stone absorb them. When you are ready, say quietly or aloud:

Spell

Worries, woes, and burdens, I release you into this stone.
I fill my cleared mind with the Moon's restorative powers.

Place the stone near a window where the Moon's cleansing energies will clear and recharge it for your next use. Do this as often as needed to keep anxiety away.

Selecting a Child's Name

Seek the Moon's guidance for just the right moniker for your little bundle of joy so that your child may live happily ever after.

Spell

Of prince, or lord, or princess be;
this royal name I seek for thee.
O' Moon of thoughtful waning light,
lend sweet help to solve this plight.
For son or daughter yet to be,
to crown you with a name that's right
To live life rich and purposefully.

Growing an Abundant Garden

Although actually planting a garden under the Moon's light can be a little impractical, seeking her blessing for a bountiful harvest is a wise and practical thing.

Spell

In fertile ground I plant the seeds for bounty at my table.
To water, weed, and nurture full with sunlight's warming food.
In Moonlight may they sleep and dream to grow each day to be
A harvest I can share and feed to answer hunger's need.

Boosting Success Ritual

When things at the office feel stalled or look like less than your planned achievements, gaze upon the Waning Gibbous Moon. It is the perfect time to stop and reflect on the best way forward on the path to success. Progress is measured in steps forward but can only be appreciated by a look back.

Spell

I've worked so hard and progress made brings pride–a hearty cheer!
But time grows old and so, I'm told, do I just sitting here.
I see the wrinkle in the plan–the speed bump was the clue.
I'll not be slowed or swayed or cowed–I dust off and resume.

Inducing Dreams

Tuck a sprig of hyacinth, lavender, or thyme under your pillow before bedtime to induce sweet dreams. Lie comfortably and visualize the dream you would like to visit you tonight. As you drift off to sleep, repeat:

Spell

With magic herbs to scent my dreams, what stories they will tell
Of meadows free and shining seas and wonders to behold.
The Moon bestows a gentle kiss and whispers in my ear,
"Sweet dreams tonight. Rest well. Sleep tight.
New day dawns bright and clear."

New Baby Blessing

Children light the home with their innocent magic in ways unanticipated. If you're thinking of growing your family, lean on this secret spell to cast a fertile wish.

Spell

It's hard to know just when the time is right for what I seek:
A tiny little you or me–my longing's at a peak.
Sweet stars and Moon, and Earth below, please listen to my prayer,
Please bless me with your fertile luck, this gift I wish to bear.

Living Joyfully

If ever you are trying to bring more joy into your life, call upon the Waning Moon. Say quietly or aloud:

Spell

O' growing Moon, enrich my world with light that I may see,
That beauty, truth, and simple joys abound from sea to sea.
The choices made of how I see mean life lived joyfully.

Safe and Warm

The Waning Moon is a time to cleanse any anger or negative emotions you may be harboring. To release negative emotion, first prepare an environment in which you feel safe and protected. You can create this by treating yourself to an act of physical and emotional self-care.

1. Prepare your favorite warm beverage.

2. Get as comfortable as possible. Wrap yourself in a blanket. Sit in your favorite spot.

3. Slowly sip your beverage. As you sip the warm liquid, focus on it warming you from the inside. Imagine the warmth melting away any areas of "cold": anger, sadness, trauma, etc.

4. Continue to focus on the warm liquid soothing you and shifting you into a place of safety and protection. After each sip, say aloud:

Spell

I am safe. I am protected.

5. Once you have reached a state of self-created safety, you can acknowledge negative elements that may have arisen this month.

6. After you acknowledge something negative, take another small sip of your beverage and say:

Spell

I am safe. I am protected.

7. Continue this process for each negative element you acknowledge.

8. At the end, finish your beverage. Then state:

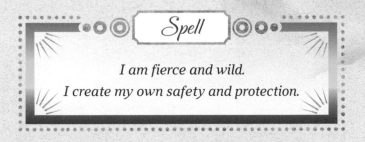

Spell

I am fierce and wild.
I create my own safety and protection.

Space of Protection Ritual

Here is how to create a space of protection inspired by a snowflake's shape and powered by the Waning Moon. Use this as a safe space for dealing with negative thoughts or other challenges.

1. Visualize drawing a shape around yourself. Stand in a quiet space and point directly in front of you. Then point directly behind you.

2. Now, as if there were an invisible semicircle connecting these points, "draw" two points by pointing at them—equally spaced between the first two points you drew—on the right side of the visualized semicircle.

3. Repeat the same thing on the left side.

4. Now connect these points by "drawing" lines with your finger as you turn around in the center, visualizing yourself connecting the points. As you draw each line, say:

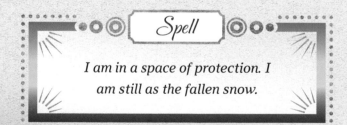

Spell

I am in a space of protection. I am still as the fallen snow.

Cleansing Your Sanctuary

There may be negativity in your home that needs to be cleansed. This phase of the lunar cycle is the right time for this act of cleansing.

What you'll need:

♦ Palo santo
♦ Fire-safe dish
♦ Flame

1. Open some doors and windows around your space to allow the smoke and negative energy to exit.

2. Light the end of the palo santo and let it burn for 60 seconds. Blow out the flame and hold the palo santo in your hand with the fire-safe dish below it to catch any falling embers.

3. Slowly walk around your space, allowing the smoke from the burned palo santo to drift upward. Periodically say:

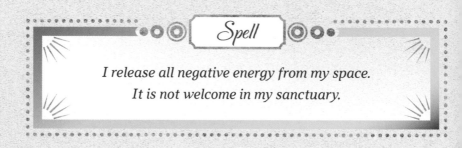

Spell

I release all negative energy from my space.
It is not welcome in my sanctuary.

4. Relight the palo santo and extinguish the flame if you need more smoke.

5. At the end of your journey, press the burned edge of the palo santo against the fire-safe dish to ensure that it is no longer burning.

6. Repeat this as often as you feel called to do so.

Letting Go

The Waning Crescent Moon is a particularly good time for letting go of things that weigh us down or just don't work in our lives the way they used to. Thank them for their service and create a space in your heart for their help, but say good-bye and move on to something that will be a positive force in your world.

Gather matches, a small sage sprig, paper, a blue or white candle, a pencil, and a small bowl of water.

1. Go to a safe place outside, under the light of the Moon, that holds special meaning for you. Light the sage to cleanse your space.

2. Light the candle and express gratitude to the Universe before writing down everything–or a specific thing–that no longer serves.

3. Take a deep breath. Exhale. Read the list quietly or aloud. Breathe in, and, as you exhale, imagine your breath carrying whatever you want to let go of away. Breathe deeply and feel a lightness, an ease, filling the negative space in you.

4. When you are ready, use the candle to light the paper (safely) and put it in the bowl of water.

Close your ritual by expressing gratitude.

Protecting
Your Loved Ones

The Waning Gibbous Moon is the Moon's first steps away from midlife into her elderly state. Instead of achieving goals, she now uses her power to nurture those she loves and wants to protect. This spell will help you pour your love and intentions into the Universe and send care to your loved ones.

What you'll need:

- Your athame
- Protection oil to anoint the candle (if you don't have one already made, use a carrier oil and rosemary)
- Three black candles for banishment
- Sage for cleansing
- Rosemary for fighting evil spirits
- Clove for protection
- Chamomile for love
- Juniper berry for protection against hexes and psychic attacks
- Bay leaves for protection
- A teapot with hot water
- Your cauldron
- Tongs
- Matches

An athame is a ceremonial blade meant to slice through energy, whether to cast a magic circle or cut through harmful energies. For this spell, you will use it for both. Cast your circle. Before lighting the candles, anoint them with a protection oil. Light them. Then, collect the herbs and put them in your cauldron, thinking of their purposes as you do so.

Next, use your pen and bay leaves to write down the names of the people you want to protect. You can write multiple names on one leaf or a single name per leaf. When writing down each set of initials, think of that person being covered in a bubble of light that nothing can burst. That light is your love and this spell.

Hold on to the leaf or leaves with the tongs and burn them on the candles' flames. Place them inside the cauldron. When you've completed each name, pour the hot water into the cauldron and inhale the herbal fragrance. Let it flow through you. Then raise your hands to the Moon and say:

Spell

Mother Moon, protect them in the way I can't.
Keep them safe and wrap them in my love.

Now, believe she will.

Releasing
and Receiving Ritual

There are moments where we may want something so badly that it consumes us. It takes over our craft, our minds, and our hearts. This obsession can tear us down if we let it. Instead of attracting our desires, we may inadvertently send them away.

The Waning Gibbous Moon is a phase in which we can release our unyielding ideas of what we should have right now and make room for what Spirit has for us. This ritual will help you open your mind and find peace again.

> What you'll need:
>
> ♦ Turquoise for clarity
> ♦ Bloodstone for honesty
> ♦ Moonstone for the connection to Mother Moon

Sit in a quiet place where you can see the Moon. Close your eyes and envision the thing you want the most. Hold on to the crystals and let them affect you. Ask yourself *why* you want this thing. What do you believe it will bring you? What do you find lacking in your life that makes you think you need it? And what will it mean if you don't get it?

Imagine yourself as a tight fist that refuses to let go. Then imagine Spirit slowly prying those fingers apart, one by one. When the fist is an open palm, say:

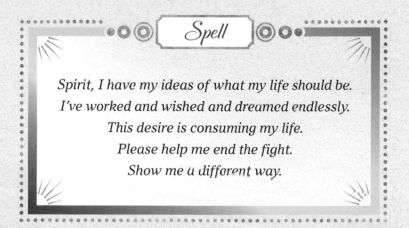

Spell

Spirit, I have my ideas of what my life should be.
I've worked and wished and dreamed endlessly.
This desire is consuming my life.
Please help me end the fight.
Show me a different way.

Listen to what Spirit says and receive it.

Managing Expectations for Yourself

With only half the Moon still illuminated, the Last Quarter Moon clearly warns that the Dark Moon is fast approaching. It's here that we should reflect on what happened during the Moon cycle, on our blessings, and on our goals and outcomes. There may be months when you've achieved everything you set out to do, and there will be months when you feel as though you accomplished nothing.

When that happens, it's easy for feelings of inadequacy or failure to slip in and wreak havoc on your confidence. Remember that there are no failures, only lessons. With the guidance of the Waning Moon and your own intuition, you can learn to correct, but more importantly, to be kind to yourself.

This spell is a form of shadow work, so cast a magic circle and write down how you're feeling about yourself–unedited. What do you think of the progress you've made so far? As you write, don't tear yourself down. Meditate on why you assigned these words to yourself. Keep those words in mind and imagine them floating around in your brain, simply existing.

Ask the Moon:

Spell

Do these words truly suit me?
Am I seeing myself clearly?
What do you see?

Allow Mother Moon to speak to you. Chances are, she won't agree with the harsh things you say about yourself. Then, one by one, imagine those words disintegrating in her light and replace them with the good that Mother Moon sees in you. Cleanse your space of bad energy, thank the Moon, and go forward, periodically harkening back to what she said. Be kind to yourself, and remember you're doing the best you can.

Reflecting and Realigning Ritual

The beauty of the Last Quarter Moon is that half of the Moon is in darkness and the other half is in light. She's a mix between contemplation and action. Most of our work has been done, and now it's time to reflect on the past month and realign ourselves after everything we've accomplished. This is our spiritual tune-up to keep us in our best mental and emotional states.

What you'll need:

♦ The Hermit tarot card
♦ The Star tarot card
♦ Four of Cups tarot card

Sit or lie back in a comfortable position. Lay the three cards in front of you, starting with The Hermit. Like you, the Hermit has been through a lot. He's achieved so much that it's taken him to the top of the mountain. In his new position, The Hermit looks down on where he started and how far he's come.

Contemplate your accomplishments and either write them down or meditate on them.

Next, focus on the Four of Cups. This is a transitional card, representing the need for introspection and evaluation. In tarot, the number four represents balance. Use this card as a reminder to take the good with the bad for overall peace. Are you holding on to a thought that doesn't serve you anymore? Contemplate it or write it down.

Last, turn your attention to The Star. This card represents rebirth and spirituality. It depicts a woman pouring water both on the land and into a lake, symbolizing the renewal of life. Seven smaller stars shine in the sky above her, representing the seven chakras. Begin from your root chakra and move all the way to your crown chakra, checking in with each chakra along the way. If your chakras are clear, so is your soul.

Take a cleansing breath and rest, knowing you've done the work.

Restoring Your Intuition

Intuition is our inner compass. It guides us when we're unsure of ourselves. It's the "gut feeling" we get about a person or situation. Everyone has it, but witches actively use it in our practices. Intuition is like a muscle that has to be used consistently or it will become weaker. Blocks to our intuition include doubt, stress, and fatigue. If we're not taking care of ourselves, our internal compass gets stuck and we get lost in the process.

The Waning Crescent is the last phase in which we're still able to get a glint of the passing moonlight and use it to restore ourselves and get back on track in time for the New Moon.

What you'll need:

♦ Iris flower for intuition
♦ Sunflower for guidance
♦ Purple candle to represent your third eye

Set and light the candle in a dark room, letting its fire be your only source of light. Place the iris to the left of you and the sunflower to your right so you're protected on both sides.

Even when we feel lost, the compass inside us still exists; it's similar to when the clouds block the Sun. Identify what is blocking your intuition. How did you get here?

Next, take three deep breaths to put yourself in a state of relaxation. Ground yourself by touching both plants at your sides. Feel their petals and take comfort knowing they're here for you. Now that you're grounded, stare into the flame and soften your focus. Nothing else exists except the light. When you're completely relaxed and entranced, say the words:

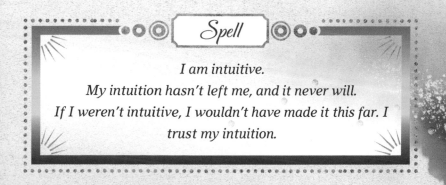

Spell

I am intuitive.
My intuition hasn't left me, and it never will.
If I weren't intuitive, I wouldn't have made it this far. I
trust my intuition.

Say it until you believe it. It is the truth.

When you are finished, say a prayer of gratitude to the flowers, to yourself, and to Mother Moon for her help.

Sleepytime Epsom Salt Soak

Right before the Dark Moon rules the skies, there's one sliver of light left. The Waning Crescent represents the Sun dipping out of sight and letting in the night. Now, the night is meant for sleep. So many of us have trouble getting to sleep and staying asleep. The stress of our everyday lives can be all-consuming, just for us to wake up and do everything all over again. But if we don't sleep, we can't be our best selves, which shows in our magic. If you don't make time for yourself to rest, certainly no one else will. Give yourself some time to soak in your tub. Sink right in.

What you'll need:

- Epsom salt for its boost of serotonin
- Lavender essential oil (or dried lavender) for healing
- Chamomile for calm
- Hibiscus for harmony
- Muslin bag
- String
- Blue candles for peace
- Blue lace agate for tranquility

Prepare this soak when you know you won't be interrupted, preferably the night before you have a day off. Turn on the water and adjust the temperature as needed. Make sure it's not too cold, or it might wake you up instead of letting you relax. Light the candles and arrange them about your bathroom where they won't burn anything. When the tub is about a third full, add the Epsom salt. If you're using lavender oil, place a few drops inside the muslin bag and then add the dried herbs. Draw the bag closed and use the string to tie it to the bath faucet so it stains the water.

When you're ready, get right in, bringing the blue lace agate with you. Now just *breathe* and enjoy yourself. You deserve this.

Conclusion

The Moon has been and will always be a gorgeous fixture in the sky. Knowing her, her beauty, her wisdom, and her influence will affect you and your practice for the rest of your life.

You've delighted in her youthful stage, learning how to plan and dream. You've grown with her and gotten clear on what you hope for yourself and others. You've thanked her for her kindness and reached your peak energy with her cheering you on. And you've rested and taken a step back at what you've accomplished, no matter how big or small. You now know what she's capable of and how she works her magic in our lives on this earth. The more you get to know her, the more she'll reveal herself to you.

Mother Moon may guide you in dream magic, in meeting with otherworldly spirits, and through every new stage in your life as you follow every step of hers. There's no end to what she can teach you, and with time, your relationship with her can grow to where you won't need to consult a calendar to know when she'll make an appearance. You'll just know.

Now that you've learned who Mother Moon is, how she can help you, and how to honor her, it's our hope that you continue to become more in tune with her until you're just as much in tune with her as you naturally are with the Sun. Let her reveal more of herself to you. This is only the beginning of your spiritual journey and your relationship with her. Keep her by your side, and she will support you.

SO MOTE IT BE.

Spell Index

4. Waning Moon Spells

First published in 2023, by Wellfleet, an imprint of The Quarto Group,
142 West 36th Street, 4th Floor, New York, NY 10018, USA
T (212) 779-4972 F (212) 779-6058 www.Quarto.com

Contains content previously published in 2020 as *Moon Magic* and *House Magic*, in
2021 as *Herbal Magic*, and in 2022 as *Goddess Magic* by Wellfleet Press, an imprint
of The Quarto Group, 142 West 36th Street, 4th Floor, New York, NY 10018

Wellfleet titles are also available at discount for retail, wholesale, promotional,
and bulk purchase. For details, contact the Special Sales Manager by email
at specialsales@quarto.com or by mail at The Quarto Group, Attn: Special Sales
Manager, 100 Cummings Center Suite 265D, Beverly, MA 01915 USA.

10 9 8 7 6 5 4 3 2 1

ISBN: 978-1-57715-391-7

Library of Congress Control Number: 2023933786

Publisher: Rage Kindelsperger
Creative Director: Laura Drew
Managing Editor: Cara Donaldson
Editor: Sara Bonacum
Cover and Interior Design: Evelin Kasikov

Printed in China

Continue your spellcraft with these additional companions:

978-1-57715-390-0   978-1-57715-392-4   978-1-57715-388-7

978-1-57715-393-1   978-1-57715-389-4